A DECADE OF POP
1980s
20 of the Best Songs
ARRANGED BY DAN COATES

CONTENTS

Produced by
Alfred Music
P.O. Box 10003
Van Nuys, CA 91410-0003
alfred.com

Printed in USA.

ISBN-10: 1-4706-3200-4
ISBN-13: 978-1-4706-3200-7

Cover Photos
Sound mixer: © gettyimages.com / tunart • Digital equalizer background: © gettyimages.com / Mikado767

AFTER ALL

Words and Music by
Dean Pitchford and Tom Snow
Arr. Dan Coates

AGAINST ALL ODDS

Words and Music by Phil Collins
Arr. Dan Coates

Slowly
Verse:

1. How can I just let you walk a-way, just let you leave with-out___ a trace? When I stand here tak - ing ev - 'ry breath with you; ooh,___ you're the on - ly one who real - ly knew me at all.___

2. How can you just walk a - way from me, when all___ I can do is watch you leave? 'Cause we
3. *See additional lyrics.*

Verse 3:
I wish I could just make you turn around,
Turn around and see me cry.
There's so much I need to say to you,
So many reasons why.
You're the only one who really knew me at all.
(To Chorus:)

ALWAYS

Words and Music by
Jonathan Lewis, David Lewis and Wayne Lewis
Arr. Dan Coates

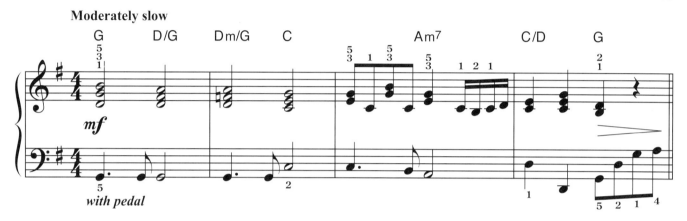

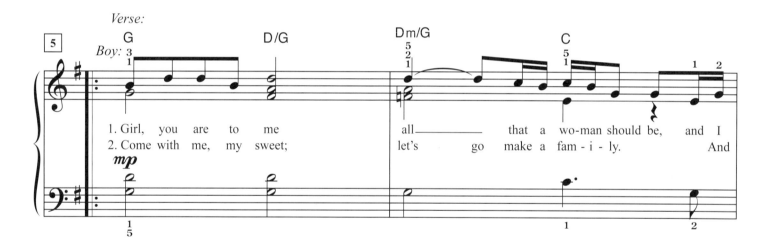

1. Girl, you are to me all_____ that a wo-man should be, and I
2. Come with me, my sweet; let's go make a fam-i-ly. And

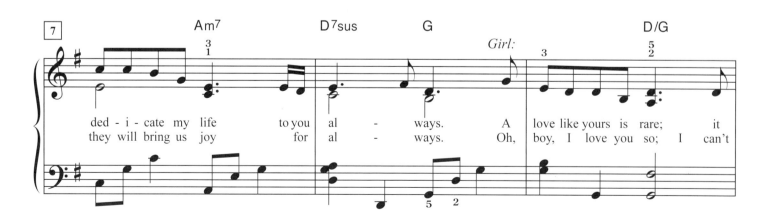

ded-i-cate my life to you al - ways. A love like yours is rare; it
they will bring us joy for al - ways. Oh, boy, I love you so; I can't

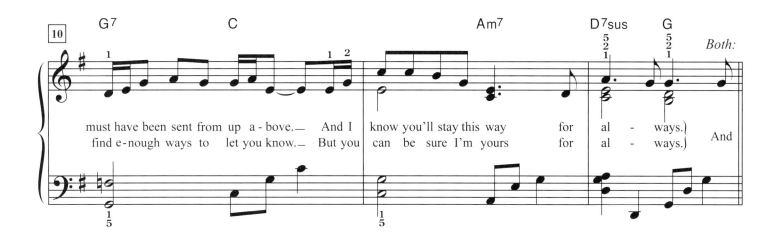

must have been sent from up a-bove.— And I | know you'll stay this way for al - ways.) | And
find e-nough ways to let you know.— But you | can be sure I'm yours for al - ways.)

Pre-Chorus:

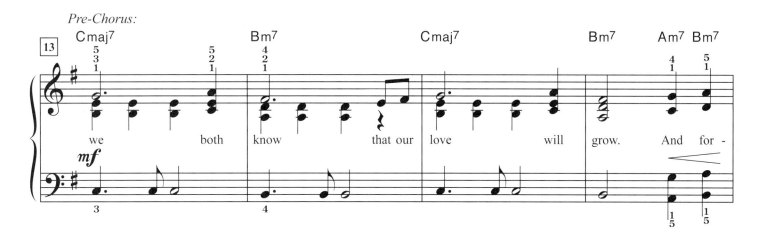

we both know that our love will grow. And for-

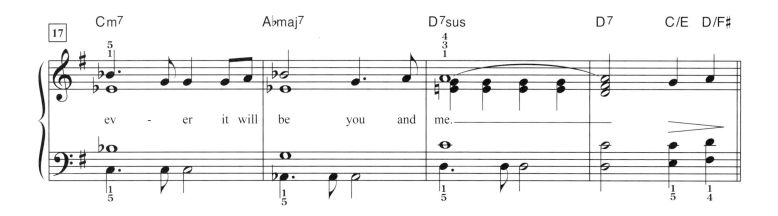

ev - er it will be you and me.—

Chorus:

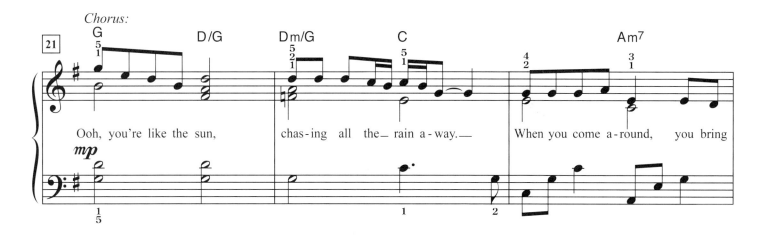

Ooh, you're like the sun, chas-ing all the— rain a-way.— When you come a-round, you bring

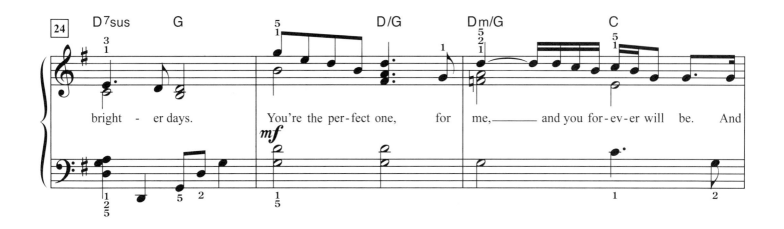

bright - er days. You're the per-fect one, for me,_____ and you for-ev-er will be. And

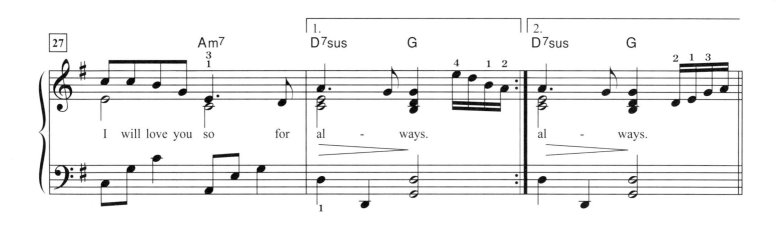

I will love you so for al - ways. al - ways.

Ooh_____ ooh - hoo. I will love you so for al - ways.

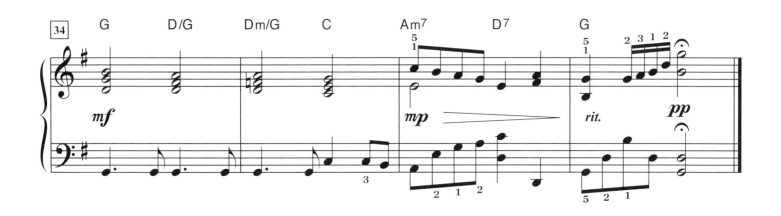

BROKEN WINGS

Words and Music by Richard Page,
Steve George and John Lang
Arr. Dan Coates

DON'T STOP BELIEVIN'

Words and Music by Jonathan Cain,
Neal Schon and Steve Perry
Arr. Dan Coates

D.S. al Coda

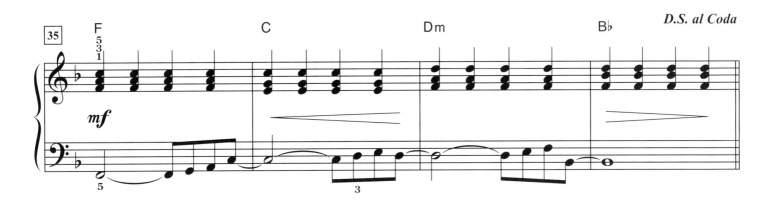

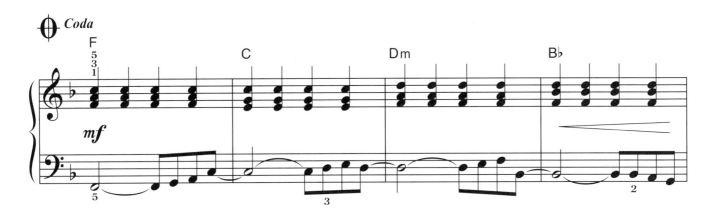

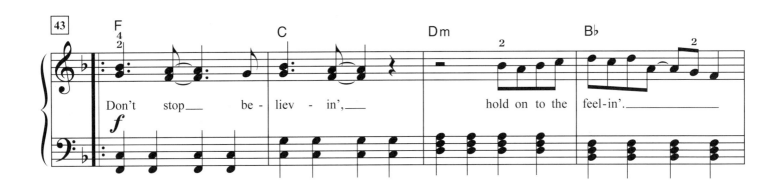

Don't stop___ be - liev - in',___ hold on to the feel-in'._____

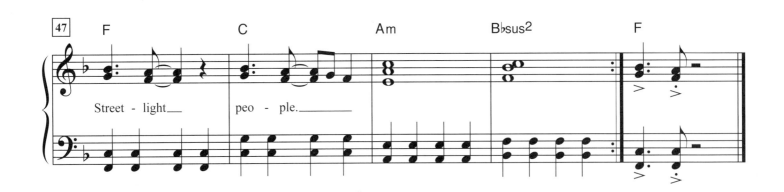

Street - light___ peo - ple._____

Verse 3:
A singer in a smoky room,
The smell of wine and cheap perfume.
For a smile they can share the night
It goes on and on and on and on.
(To Chorus:)

Verse 4:
Working hard to get my fill.
Everybody wants a thrill,
Payin' anything to roll the dice
Just one more time.
(To Verse 5:)

Verse 5:
Some will win and some will lose,
Some were born to sing the blues.
Oh, the movie never ends,
It goes on and on and on and on.
(To Chorus:)

EYE OF THE TIGER

(from *Rocky III*)

Words and Music by
Frankie Sullivan III and Jim Peterik
Arr. Dan Coates

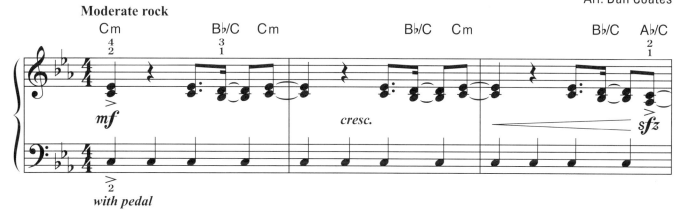

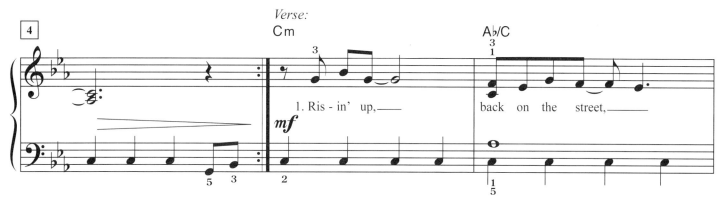

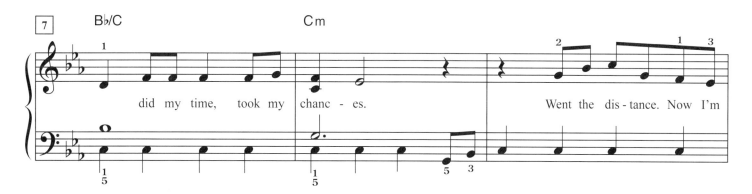

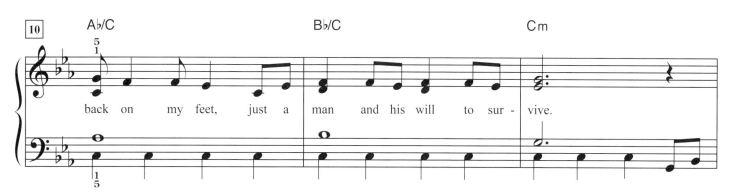

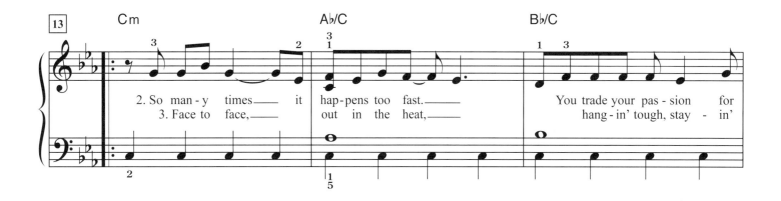

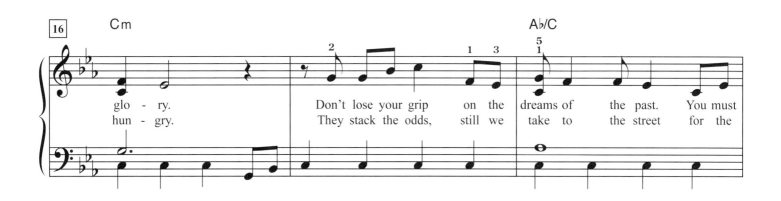

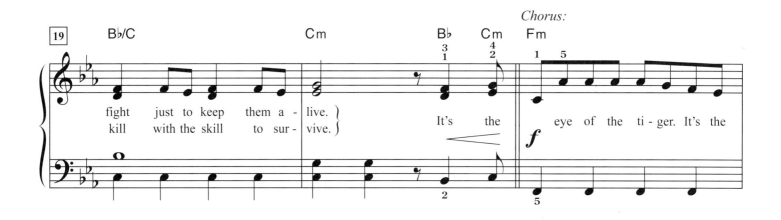

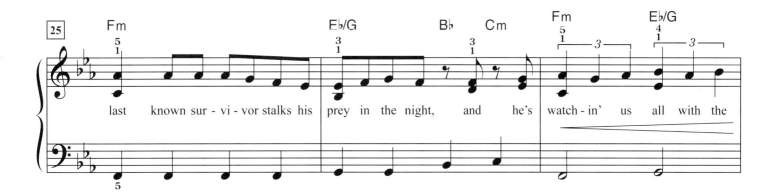

last known sur - vi - vor stalks his prey in the night, and he's watch - in' us all with the

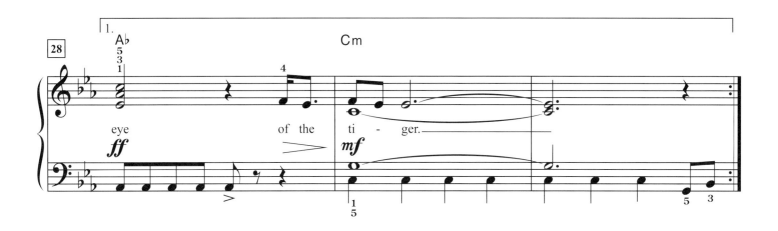

eye of the ti - ger.

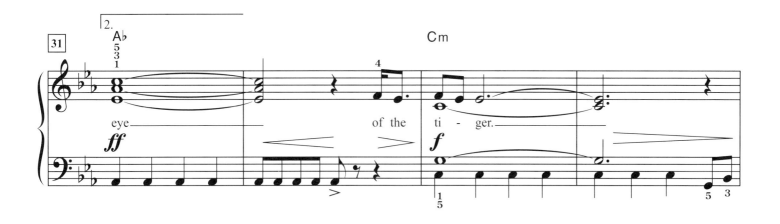

eye of the ti - ger.

ENDLESS LOVE

Words and Music by Lionel Richie
Arr. Dan Coates

FAITHFULLY

Words and Music by Jonathan Cain
Arr. Dan Coates

Moderately slow

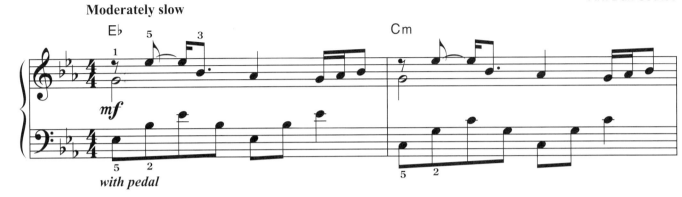

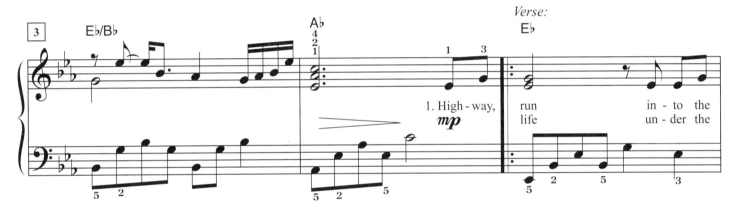

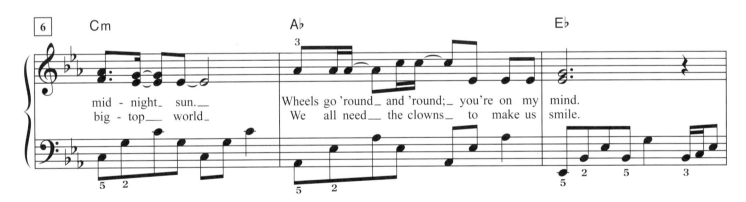

faith - ful - ly.

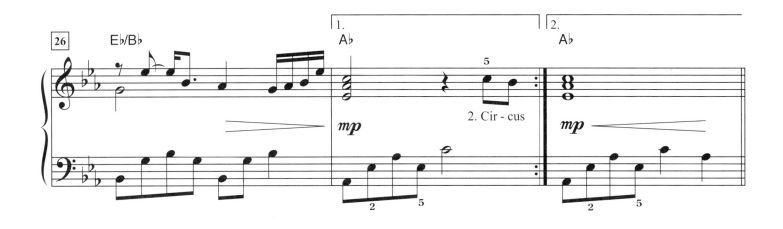

2. Cir - cus

Oh,   oh,

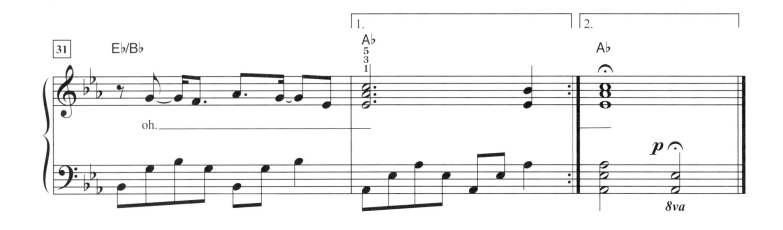

oh.

8va

GLORY OF LOVE
(from *The Karate Kid, Part II*)

Words and Music by David Foster,
Peter Cetera and Diane Nini
Arr. Dan Coates

Verse 3:
You keep me standing tall,
You help me through it all,
I'm always strong when you're beside me.
I have always needed you,
I could never make it alone.
(To Chorus:)

GREATEST LOVE OF ALL

Words by Linda Creed
Music by Michael Masser
Arr. Dan Coates

KOKOMO

Words and Music by Mike Love,
Scott McKenzie, Terry Melcher and John Phillips
Arr. Dan Coates

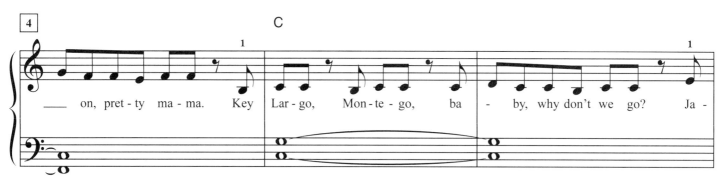

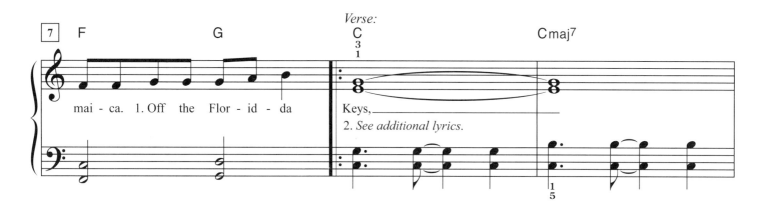

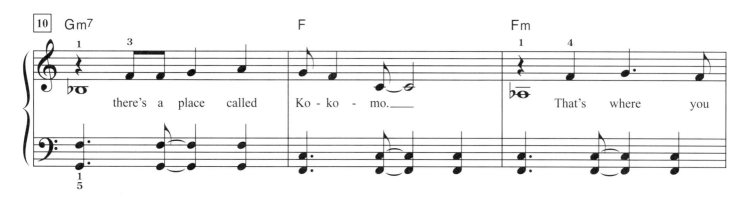

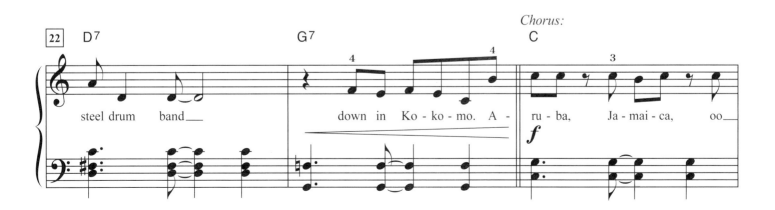

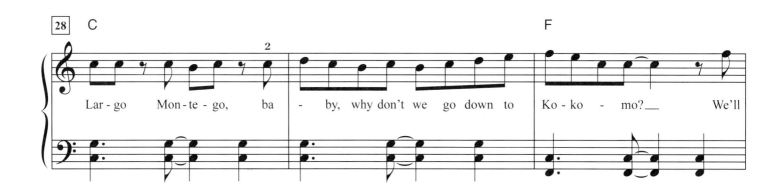

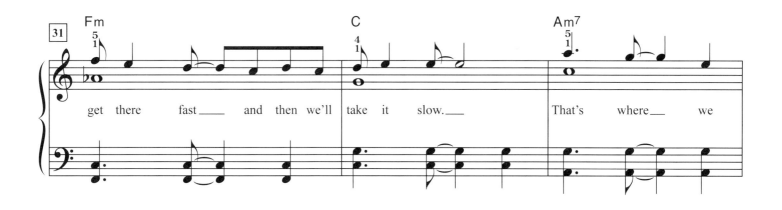

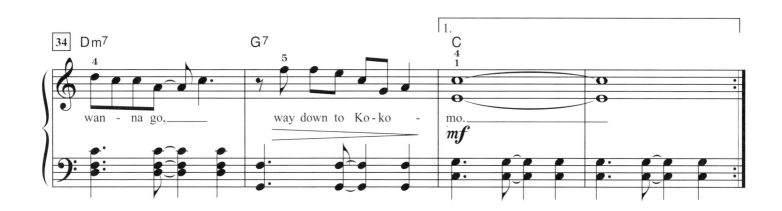

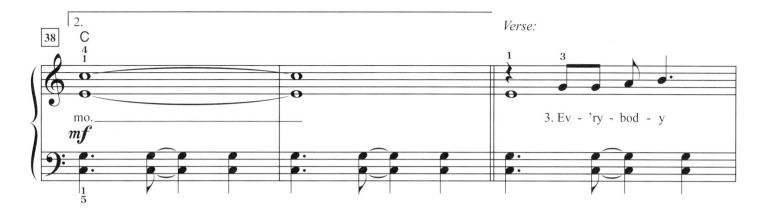

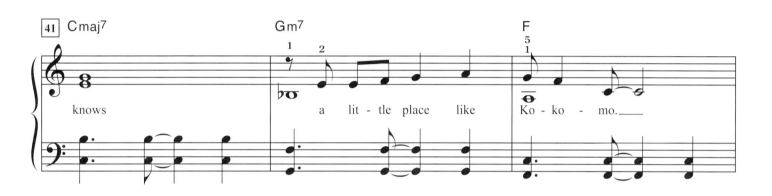

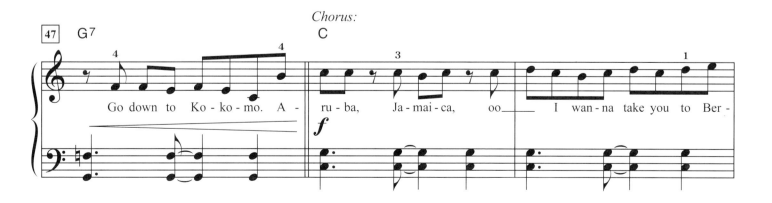

Verse 2:
We'll put out to sea,
And we'll perfect our chemistry.
And by and by
We'll defy a little bit of gravity.
Afternoon delight,
Cocktails and moonlit nights.
The dreamy look in your eye,
Give me a tropical contact high
Way down in Kokomo.
(To Chorus:)

LOOK AWAY

Words and Music by Diane Warren
Arr. Dan Coates

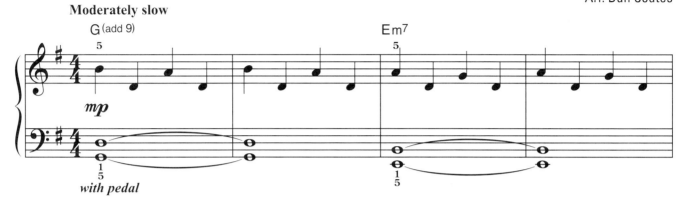

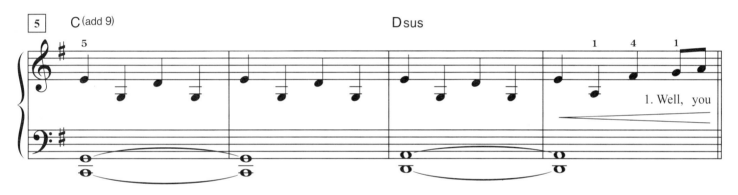

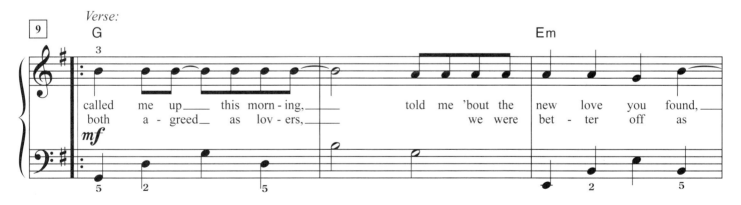

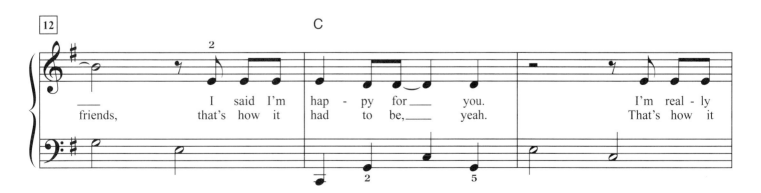

MORNING TRAIN
(9 to 5)

Words and Music by Florrie Palmer
Arr. Dan Coates

OPEN ARMS

Words and Music by
Jonathan Cain and Steve Perry
Arr. Dan Coates

RHYTHM OF THE NIGHT

Words and Music by Diane Warren
Arr. Dan Coates

Verse 2:
Look out on the street now,
The party's just beginning.
The music's playing;
A celebration's starting.
Under the street lights,
The scene is being set.
A night for romance,
A night you won't forget.
So come join the fun,
This ain't no time to be staying home,
Ooh, there's too much going on.
Tonight is gonna be a night like you've never known.
We're gonna have a good time the whole night long, oh.
(To Chorus:)

TAKE MY BREATH AWAY

Music by Giorgio Moroder
Words by Tom Whitlock
Arr. Dan Coates

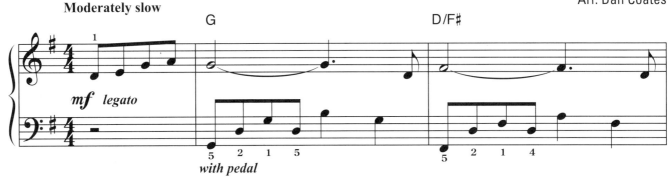

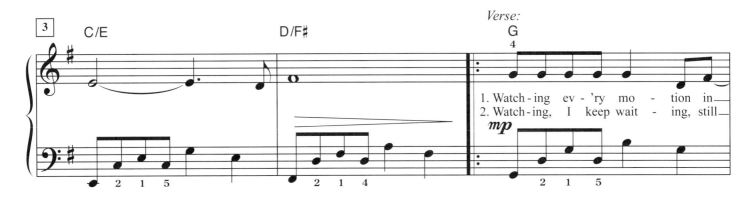

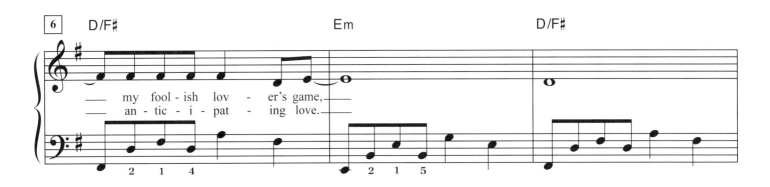

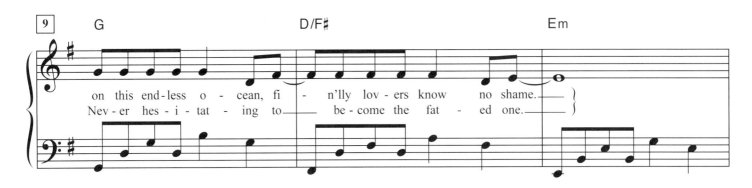

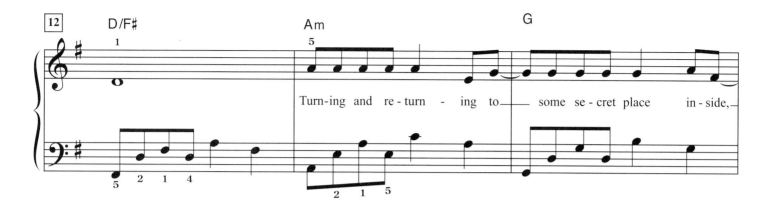

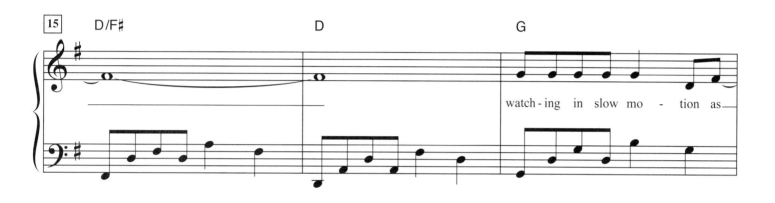

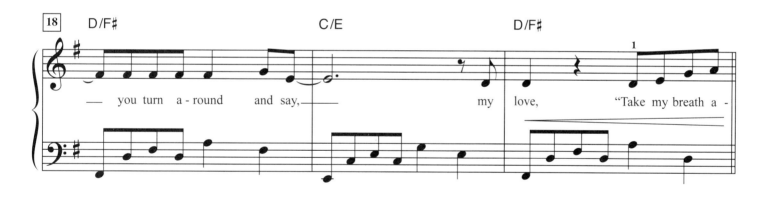

Take my breath a - way."

dim.

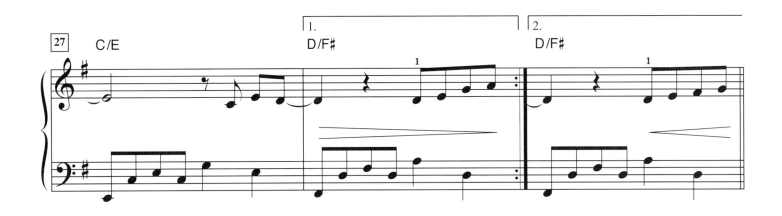

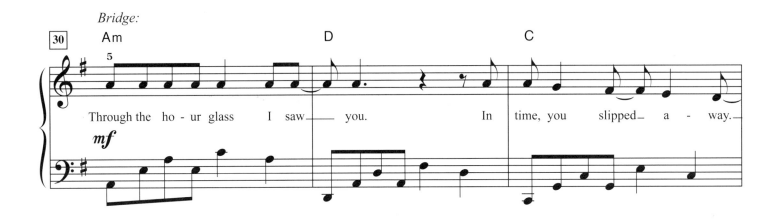

Bridge:

Through the ho - ur glass I saw⎯ you.   In time, you slipped⎯ a - way.⎯

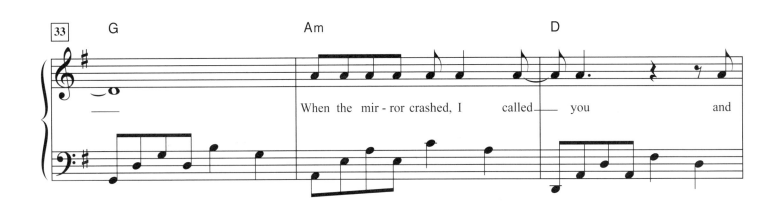

⎯   When the mir - ror crashed, I called⎯ you   and

turned to hear— you say,——— "If on-ly for to-day,——————

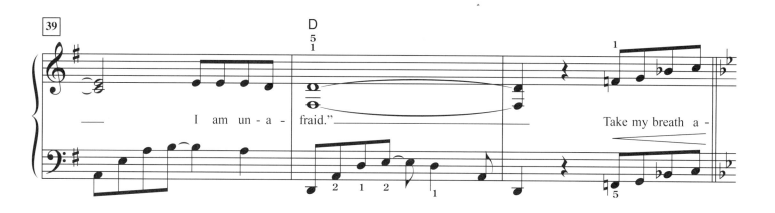

——— I am un-a-fraid."——————— Take my breath a-

Chorus:

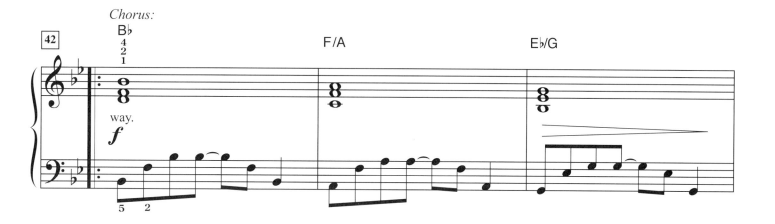

way.

Take my breath a-   *rit. e dim.*

THAT'S WHAT FRIENDS ARE FOR

Music by Burt Bacharach
Words by Carole Bayer Sager
Arr. Dan Coates

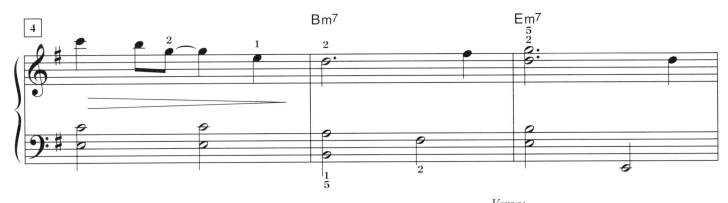

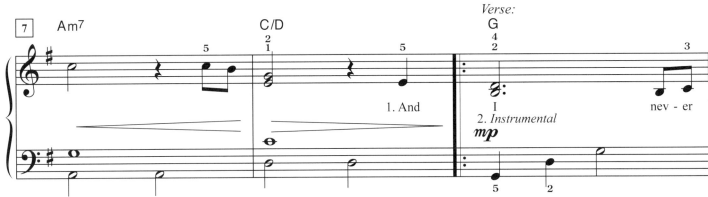

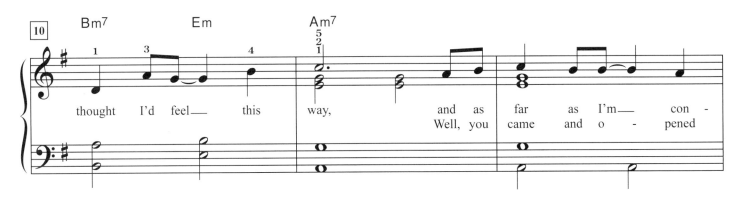

WHO'S THAT GIRL

Words and Music by
Madonna Ciccone and Pat Leonard
Arr. Dan Coates

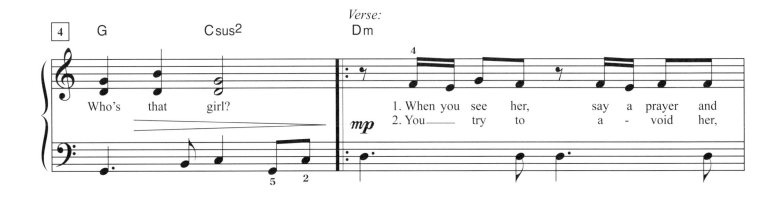

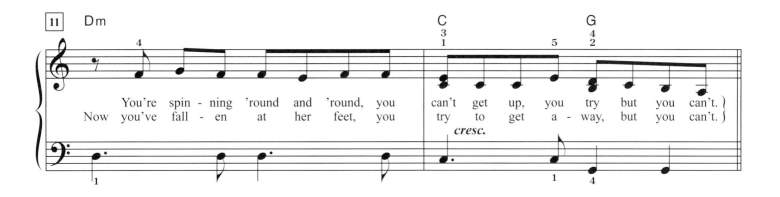

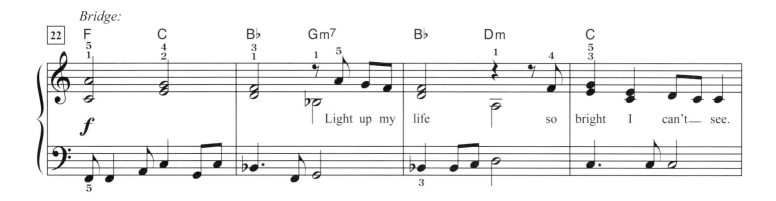

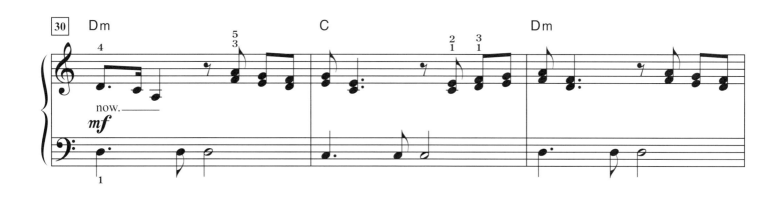

D.S. al Coda

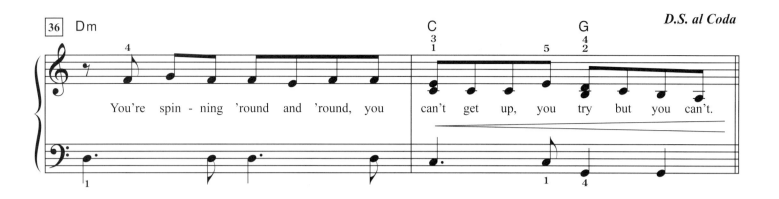

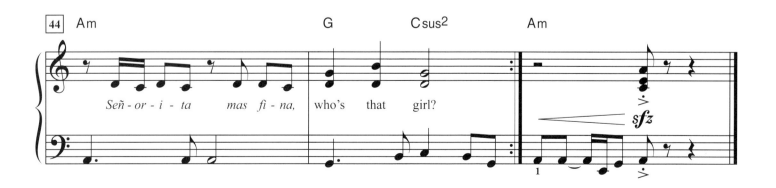

WIND BENEATH MY WINGS

(from *Beaches*)

Words and Music by
Larry Henley and Jeff Silbar
Arr. Dan Coates

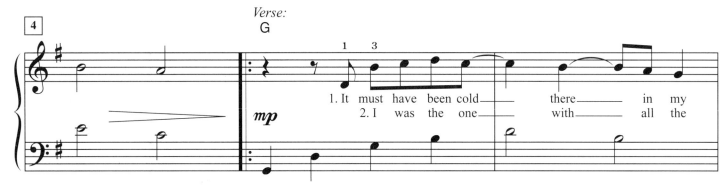

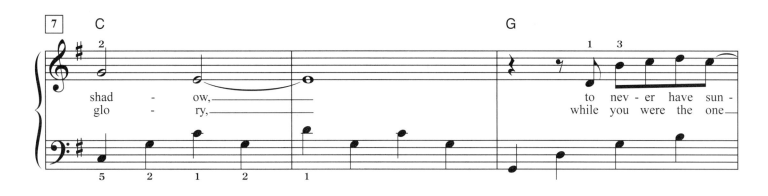

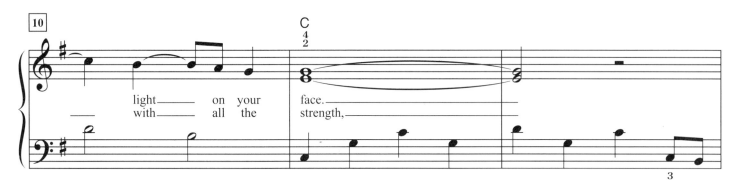

WORDS GET IN THE WAY

Words and Music by Gloria Estefan
Arr. Dan Coates

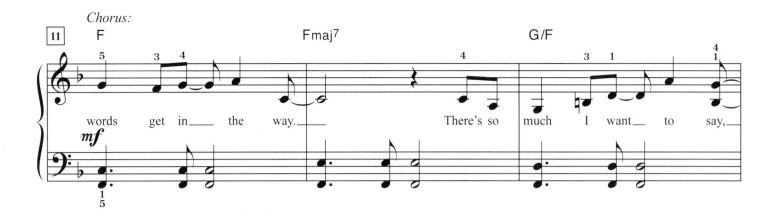

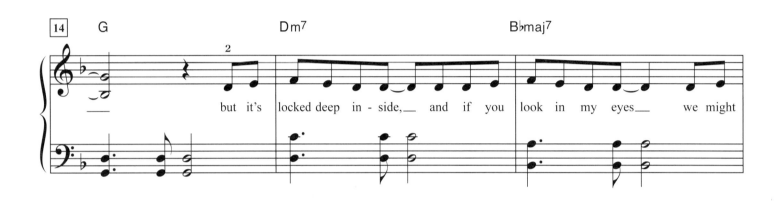

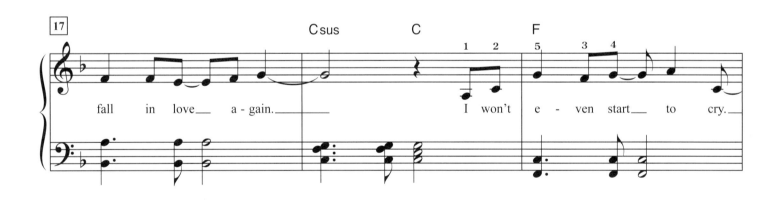

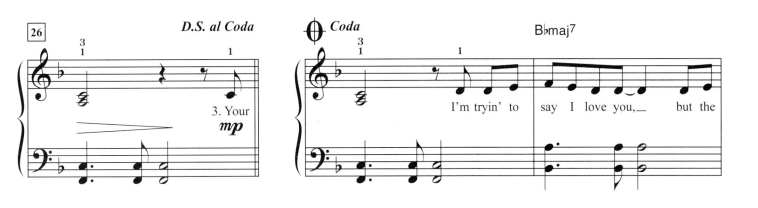

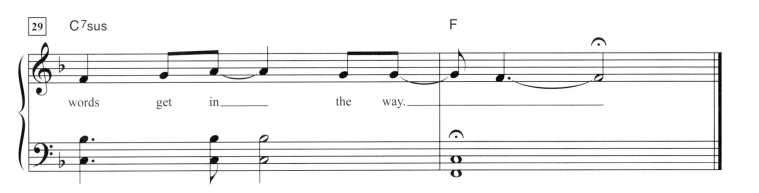

Verse 2:
But I know when you have something on your mind.
You've been tryin' to tell me for the longest time.
And before you break my heart in two,
There's something I've been tryin' to say to you.
(To Chorus:)

Verse 3:
Your heart has always been an open door.
But, baby, I don't even know you anymore.
Despite the fact it's hurting me,
I know the time has come to set you free.
(To Chorus:)